THE
PRELUDE

MARTY CAIN

Action Books   Notre Dame, IN   2023

Action Books

Joyelle McSweeney and Johannes Göransson, Founding Editors

Katherine Hedeen and Paul Cunningham, Managing Editors

Augusta Beaver and Alaina Johansson, Editorial Assistants 2022–2023

Jeffrey Angles, Daniel Borzutzky, Don Mee Choi, Advisory Board

Shanna Compton, Book Design

First Edition

ISBN: 978-0-900575-16-7

Library of Congress Control Number: 2022949873

Cover art: Shanna Compton, *The Green Room* (2023). Digital mixed media.

For more information, please contact us at

Action Books, 233 Decio Hall, Notre Dame, IN 46556

or visit

actionbooks.org

for Mae

Who loves the sun?

—The Velvet Underground

May prose and property both die out
And leave me peace

—Lorine Niedecker

The Contents of This Work, produced at the confluence of Several Bodies of Water Both Moving and Not:

Over time, I learned that the creek had an unconscious. In the summertime, covered in sweat, in the void of diversion, we spoke to each other. This is what it said to me.

BOOK FIRST

Introduction—Residence in the Subgarden

A fractal beholden. A plug of time.
To rot or wonder
To amble and wander
To stand at the crest of the schoolyard
When the wind comes running, the milk
Soaks slowly into the whitebread sandwich
Of youthful absence and comes
At night like a red stream on the floor still
And drips through the cracks onto
The schnauzer in the apartment downstairs
One eye open, a vision creeps
Under the door, forms on fire
Leaking from each hole wrung from here
To the coming Monday. Does the leather hold
At the end of the form. Can it contain hay
Or does straw lose meaning. It still arises
In dreams of delinquent fields
Of cattails slamming your body
As you wander lonely
As a feather or corpse dog of longing
When I remove the head
It sputters orange on the floor
You call the cops. I go to work
I look in the creek
I see my body
It's not my body
I stop mine time
I annotate mine eye

EVERY LIVING THING REPLACES THE ABSENCE OF EVERY OTHER LIVING THING

a garden littered with thousands of stomachs, the crows
 hovering and endlessly pecking . . .

it is 3 o'clock. the luxury condos rupture the Commons
& the stomachs pulsate—

O ROLL ON OVER

the birds peck deeper
and inside one stomach is Sun
circling the tube with a red ribbon
and I inject it . . .

it swims in my rivers
            and my eyes open like tiny mouths
eating scenery and ferns sprout from ears and
         slash my throat and a fungus grows from the chasm
both presence and absence are interminable fictions
yet power lives on within one body in the dark & I gaze
through the window and see myself slash my arm
the torrent of blood splatters the glass

MY SILVERY TOOTH / MY PRIVATE SELF

the teeth were a symbol of capital gathered
and seeing myself feed himself and yourself
I meet his eyes, the Chainsawer of Sun
I meet my mouth with silver lips

prime the motor

- -

HOW TO FEEL ALIVE / WITHOUT TURNING AWAY

to feel alive and love the sun without relinquishing the shadowy spots on the lawn
                              & moving our chairs closer to the light

like a cat napping its way down the hall
       every twenty minutes as we sipped on juleps
we'd taken mushrooms in the morning
           the wasp nests hum like lungs on the roof
             and the sun was a prism
                     the wind & the violence
                  I know them well
                  I know the Chainsawer is a seer
             I know he was born in June & died in August
       I know he has fruit and vegetable organs
and inhabits a murk of fern seedlings and rare mineral patterns
       in a space
           I call the subgarden
       a meadow the Menace has tried to poison
they lay down orange peels and pennies to try and catch it
they pour down Drano to try and kill it

[A BRIEF PAUSE]

when the man comes into my home to unclog the system he leaves grease stains on every
imaginable surface

[I STUDY THE TRACE]

the smell of a corpse on the second floor
or of alcohol eating the body within

I have never smelled death

when he left I looked in the toilet bowl
I saw a ball of hair in fluorescent light

for a nest of lines it makes a form
I pull them out one by one to rest
on the humid wall of ceramic tiles
a failing motion / an archival impulse

I grip the ball
It foams & shrieks within my hand

ONE WAY TO BITE BACK: IF SYSTEM IS
ORGANIC, BECOME ALCOHOL & FOMENT
DEATH OVERWHELMING THE PROSAIC
FUNCTION OF ORGANS TO ROT OUT THE
BEAMS WHICH COMPRISE THE HOTEL THE
INFRASTRUCTURE SLOWLY ERODING UPON
EXPOSURE TO DRANO

NOTICE:
Matter
Separates
Over
Time

The Drano, upon entering the plumbing of the subgarden—a complex system of tunnels that have run through the sedimented rock layers for generations—is a threat to the local subgarden flora and fauna, causing forms of violence that alternate between degradation and horrific mutation. The native Sun Mare, for example, undergoes a disjoining of the genesis host (the Horse Creature) from its adoptive Child (the Preteen Boy). The stomach splits, rendering the Preteen Boy a fluid that soaks into the soil of the subgarden, having adverse effects upon plant growth, and consequently, communal forms of agricultural subsistence. Within subgarden communities, Drano is considered to be a form of chemical warfare, and is a frequent tool of the Menace in its police and military raids.

❊   ❊   ❊   ❊   ❊   ❊   ❊

❊   ❊   ❊   ❊   ❊   ❊

❊   ❊   ❊   ❊   ❊   ❊   ❊

❊   ❊   ❊   ❊   ❊   ❊

a beautiful enclosure

the law decrees the inside. the law decrees the outside. it regulates the inconsequential difference between the pig's exterior and its hygienic innards, a randomly generated system of blue pipes branching off in various directions. the thicket is inside. the meadow is thick. the chasm is outside. the grotto is inside, the bands of children cluster around garbage on fire eating lunchables and bedazzling jackets. when the law crushes the skull of the deer on the highway, dragging it to the shoulder in the interest of public safety, the gnatcloud erupts and the division between "center" and "periphery" momentarily ruptures as its pyloric artery splits and fluid congeals with cigarette butts and sediment. the deer becomes infrastructure—a bridge, a guardrail, a bottomless tunnel—then disappears, neither outside nor in.

[I will love you on the outside. I will love you within.]

when you read this, according to the law, you are reading the "inside," a dichotomy that retains coherence through the presence of various formal traits: a cover; a barcode; an author; a spine.

by form, I mean: the tangible entities that separate meaning from obliteration.

I would like to die. I would like for you to grasp the nearest sharp object, forcing it into the meat of the spine and pushing until the object emerges on the other side of the text in the fashion of a groundhog gingerly sniffing the air. this is not meant to be a violent gesture. this is what the state does, the holy punctum, what breathing does, what the law of scent does when the allergens cross borders and occupy sentries and the wriggling snouts of dogs. this is a form, an inscription, a cresting of light across the water to reveal the corpse that rests at the bottom.

you stick in your hand. you open the corpse:

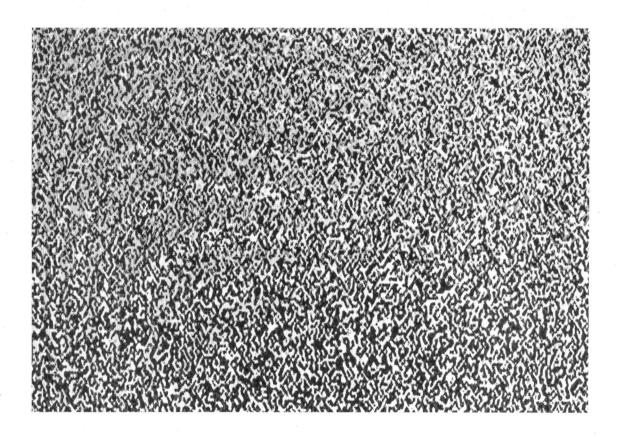

a squirrel resides in exhaust pipe metal, I woke up thinking. a vulture cloud like opening credits a knife a bruise a voice says *make babies* a prelude to walking up and smelling the rain was blue lightning in the forest around us to scrape dirt from my ornery chest a cavity of silence a small toothache of the heart or jaw or febrile jowl sewing my eyes shut to think of summer like pork necks dreaming under plastic wrap I CAN'T GET RECEPTION the depression molded into edible noodles or write in the winter living in the three-foot radius of a space heater the candle a button undone the sweating brow a small animal living all over the skin a beaver nest of feeling to foment and explode across the cubicle desk the cubist rainbow in the provincial country the unfiltered form of the deer opened up the ecstatic vein the season of shaking yourself asleep. I woke up thinking

HOW MUCH OF THIS
~~IS TIME THEFT~~
~~IS TIME WASTED~~
AGAINST TIME

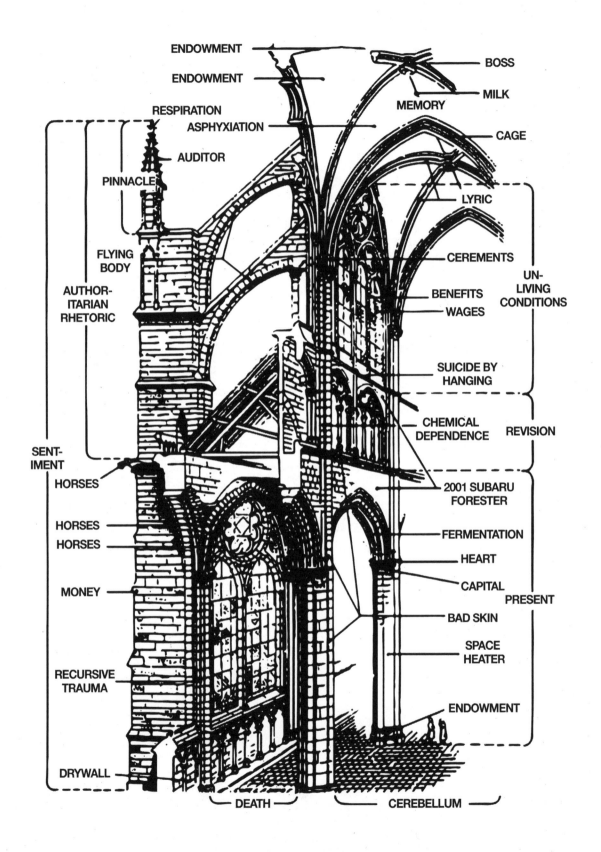

ENDOWMENT

ENDOWMENT

BOSS

MILK

MEMORY

RESPIRATION

ASPHYXIATION

CAGE

AUDITOR

PINNACLE

LYRIC

CEREMENTS

FLYING BODY

BENEFITS

WAGES

AUTHOR-ITARIAN RHETORIC

UN-LIVING CONDITIONS

SUICIDE BY HANGING

CHEMICAL DEPENDENCE

REVISION

SENT-IMENT

HORSES

2001 SUBARU FORESTER

HORSES

FERMENTATION

HORSES

HEART

MONEY

CAPITAL

PRESENT

BAD SKIN

SPACE HEATER

RECURSIVE TRAUMA

ENDOWMENT

DRYWALL

DEATH

CEREBELLUM

BOOK SECOND

The Fall of the State—Nature's Certain Course

& meanwhile, nightcrawlers wriggle on . . .

beneath the subgarden, a cosmic vein, a metallic fuselage from which mutated weeds grow . . .

I'm in the basement beneath a halogen bulb. I'm in the cellar, pulling the cord of the generator at a rhythmically acceptable rate and when the room lights up, specters surround me & the walls bleed a skeleton fluorescent, a wire runs from the sun into the back of my skull and I develop antidotes to the desire to harm myself and others. check this box. open this drawer. flick this switch. stretch the elastic around your ears so they distend like elephantic wings of a grackled brain. the nightcrawlers continue, a fruitless vision of ambiguous churning subterranean labor or whatever chronologically suspect movement enters and escapes the continually stewing realm of the body. this is occupied, here. now. and the nightcrawlers wriggle, a vision of a headless figure barking orders and another person is disappeared in the embryonic night. the walls bleed, the veins emerge, they engorge and collapse and the nightcrawlers continue from the earth to the hand to the beak to the bowels to the earth to the hand to the beak to the lips.

rainwater pool. I don't want to kill myself under cloud cover.

I pray to the sun
I pray to the body
I pray to the poem
Fated to murder
The reader
I receive a missive
Via the mirror
The soap bar lifts
On its own accord
And writes in script
THE COMING DAY
WILL BE YOUR LAST
There's a killer
In this sentence
In this shack
In this mall
Where we burrowed a home
And bathed in the fountain
In this garden
In this codex
Staying open

Wordsworth's brain buoyant in fluid, the jar on the shelf with light shining through. I dump it onto the operating table; it makes a "splat" and releases liquid. I ready the knives. What's it thinking when I finger the creases, what isolated universe in that mass, absorbent and fresh, the foam leaving our mouths when we touch the page and enter the hive. I stab the cerebellum and relish the breeze. I do some digging, I spread the folds. There's a Fitbit embedded within the pink; it measures the precise speed of the ambulatory lyric and provides an output of the QUANTIFIABLE AFFECTIVE RESPONSE to the epiphanic gesture that sputters the line, permeates the meadow, rides the wind like a cremated child into the cave where the prophetic words are written in a youthful cursive, neon green; the feeling machine uploads the data. It glowers in hardware and the centuries pool. I touch the brain and close my eyes, hear country music softly in the frontal cortex. I slice the brain I make a liverwurst sandwich.

[AS IF ADMONISHED FROM ANOTHER WORLD]

MULTIPLE VISIONS OF EMBODIED EXPERIENCE: 1) DIVING FOR A GEM AT THE DEPTH OF A LAKE; 2) LIVING IN THE CORPSE THAT FLOATS ON THE SURFACE INSIDE THE ORGANS SEIZING AND BLOATING AND BECOMING NOTHING, POLLEN ON WATER, A CARNATION GROWN FROM THE BASE OF THE THROAT TO EMBRACE DISORDER & THE GIG EMPLOYEES WERE PISSING IN BOTTLES, THE DESK FANS BLOWING FROM EACH DIRECTION, A SKIMMER BETWEEN THEM, A BODY QUARTERED MAKES ONLY MORE BODIES WITH FUNGAL GROWTHS THAT SEIZE UPON ON HITHERTO UNINHABITED FLESH AND ROOT AND BURST INTO FUMES THAT PRODUCE MORE BODIES. I CHEW THE LIP TO PROCURE SOME BLOOD. MY ROOT IN THE COUNTRY IS CONTINUALLY MOVING! THE WORDS WERE A BOX WITH NOTHING IN IT.

had a panic attack. fell asleep. had a dream that the used bookstore was getting rid of the poetry section. they needed more shelf space, and "poetry sucks" says the clerk at the front desk. woke up. had another panic attack. smoked a joint. listened to *The Prelude* audiobook with a Scottish narrator and walked down to the creek & Words Occupied My Brain

Wordsworth:

>   *or, haply, tired of this,*
> *To shut thine eyes and by internal light*
> *See trees, and meadows, and thy native stream*
> *Far distant—*

FUCK THE FREE MARKET
for Nick

I insert the memory card
into the neon pinkish brain

                                    I signal across the pit of time

                        & translate the past like a torrent

            -ial dust blown from the nintendo cartridge or the split-open turkey neck or the
exploded glass from the maw of the overturned police truck

                        a superhighwaycacophony metropolis broke the night

                        & the gored-open moose becomes a prismatic language
through which light moves

                                    I is dilation, I
                        is turned inward internally through the seam

of my skull I pull the ripcord to the sun's other side

                        to make a yolkier inverted I

IS AN ARTIFICIAL LAKE
is a RIVERED UNCONSCIOUS

            constructed through detonation, a highway

                    a mess hall or civilized ruby sliver
blood-adorned & preserved in the sap

                                        TO SIGNAL ACROSS

and to dig hallowed violence out from the resin

                            a blistered surface, the eye?

it's a pustule, a harvested poisonous berry from which

                            the other drips & finds difficulty

                            & I is the dying brother in the ruby anarchistic surface

& the creek mirroring the shape of the poem

I stick my feet in it

                            I STICK MY FEET IN IT

& make a more skin-like language,

///

          /   /
                    /   /
/   /   /   /   /

///

                                              & to me, that's an acre

                                          that's a projection of space

                                    that's a violent solidification of time

                              in the crystallized life of rational movement

And now the pandiculation. And now the orgiastic bluebird qualifier. And now incise the tips from my fingers. And now grow back the nails. And now ambivalent ambient space. And now inky interior birds. And now how my stomach was a mirror of the world. And now how my moss it lived in my belly. And now how the frail meadow was nonexistent. And now what was crazy they called symptomatic. And now what was crazy lived in the subgarden. And now the subgarden was Down Below. And now the subgarden was neither mother nor monster. And now I adorn mine skin with leathery moths.

WHAT I TRANSCRIBE I DO BADLY

The gleaming beauty of
The chicken headless. What's it thinking
As it moves in circles of its own shit
To wander with no brain a poem
Like canned chunky soup
And unidentifiable expired meat
The stake in the brook interrupted
By the viability of regulating currents
I shortchange the lint
To hear Sun in wind
I die on and on
Is there a center to what I'm saying
A regional arboreal
Or sociohistorical context
Framing the dewy utterance
Fuck you
The house fissured a single
Light in the garage workshop to break
A skin of shingles
The rain is a process and has an unconscious
The authoritarian density of bread
And Sun in each bubble
It self-services in several miles of wire
The agitated reflective hose
I fell in love with a leafy trap, a grave
To slip into the meadow
I rolled my ankle
While writing it down

*   *   *   *   *   *   *

  *   *   *   *   *   *

*   *   *   *   *   *

  *   *   *   *   *   *

I put my hand through the garden. I learned that it had no ending, no second side; it was a mossy crystal; it was a hive against dualism; it was a surface through which Time shined and crossed other surfaces.

I thought of this as I was standing at the bank of the river, surrounded by garments—denim, corduroy, sequined pleather, tweed—seeing my reflection and hearing myself (the wind thru the ferns like an Aeolian harp).

Does death, or this page, have a surface? Can a corpse have an ending?

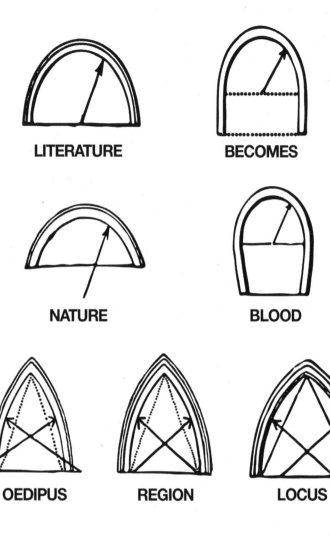

LITERATURE

BECOMES

NATURE

BLOOD

OEDIPUS

REGION

LOCUS

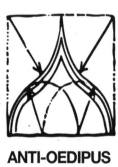

ANTI-OEDIPUS

SUBGARDEN
INSURRECTION

THE LIQUID WAS MADE AN ELECTRIFIED PLANE, A SHEET UPON WHICH FISH-CORPSES HOVER. I INJECTED CAPITAL INTO MY ARM. AN ORANGE CAPSULE SEWN IN THE SEAT OF A VAN, THE TRAUMA PRODUCED THROUGH INTERSTATE ACCESS. A RAILROAD VEIN. IS UTOPIA A COMPANY TOWN, A COUNTRY STORE, A SHEEPLAND OF RUIN. DO NARCOTICS COUNT AS A TOURIST ECONOMY. THE MEN ON SUNDAY WITH SUITCASES IN HAND. GAZE IN THE WATER. SPLICED INTO LANGUAGE AND THE RIBBON BENEATH IT. THE WOOL GLITTERS: THE SEA IS ENDLESS.

BOOK THIRD

Country Death (I Dont Hate It!)

IN THE COUNTRY

Everyone we knew from high school got addicted to heroin
or innovative multilevel marketing solutions
or suicide

·

The rain was unrelenting

·

The sun turned itself inside out

·

We stood in a lot at night & drank wine from a box

·

We sat on rotting logs on our rotting asses
smoking pouches of rotting tobacco

·

We heard the train

·

The ferns encircled our ankles and pulled us in

You get on your bike in the afternoon. You ride into the woods. You ride through the stream. You ride past the rusted frying pan hanging from the dried-out arm of the deciduous tree, humming "Every Rose Has Its Thorn" as you pop a wheelie. You come into the clearing. You come to a house with no driveway, with no mailbox, with boarded-up windows and the roof falling in, a woman in a red dress lying on her back, a hat on her face, a belt on the ground, her white skin the color of wool or some oily garment. You turn around and bike into the dark

EASY.   *PATIENT.*   *FORM.*   *COMPOSING.*

- -

The older boy on the other side of the dirt road, where you live, riding his bike shirtless. You sit on the waterbed in the echoey basement. He is your babysitter. He plays Resident Evil. You watch him play. You sit in your treehouse. You feel the wind. *A dick*, he says, *is a whale's penis.* You play with Scotch tape. You put it on his lips. He starts taking pills. When you leave for the weekend, he breaks into your family's home and your mind is a camera following inky footprints that appear on their own: DVD player, stereo, TV, Dell laptop to give his girlfriend, Mitsubishi car, drive into town, hold up the 7-11, ditch the car and steal another, high-speed chase, go to jail, steal a snowmobile, go to jail

MARE / SUN

The preteen boy walks to the barn
It is night
It is raining
He opens the door
He opens the barn door and steps inside
He takes a red rag
From a hook on the wall
He dries off his face
It leaves streaks of oil
He looks in the puddle
He sees his eyes
He climbs the rafters
He swings on the rope
He leaps into hay
He buries himself
He smells the dung
He smells the dung and pretends he lives
In some kind of chrysalis
With sun coursing through errant cracks
A shell slowly crackling as he moves his leg
A rat scurries by
How he never experienced extreme darkness
And only a purple thunder
Of one's squinted eyes
Drifting to sleep and shifting
To a different way of viewing things
The sound of a truck motor humming
And rooms melting into one another
He squints in this moment
And dreams of dying

The hay starts to itch
He digs himself out
And strands cling to his jacket
The mare is asleep
He walks to the mare
The mare is sleeping
With its eye half open
The bones locked in
A standing position
Which he knows is so
She can run when threatened
He has been threatened
In dreams and waking
By boys who are larger
Who brandish knives
And have yellow nails
Pressed against him
He walks to the mare
And lies alongside her
Caked in mud
He closes his eyes
He imagines a pink thunder
Rising from his chest
And reaching the horse
The time passes by
The thunder spirals
And becomes a ribbon
And thickens to a cord
In his dream the cord extends
From his body to the horse
And out of her mouth
And into the rafters
And into the sun

The cord is fluid
And so is he
The horse she opens
Via a crease extending
The length of her body
A piñata sawed open
He remembers the birthdays
The face in the pillow
The tears and saliva
He enters the mare
He lives in the mare
Her insides are purple
His eye is her eye
Their eyes are a marble
With yellowy waves
That go on like that
When he exhales
She gallops
And they sleep that way
And they live that way
Lying down
They smell of manure
A pail of spilled milk
A trough of Time
Their body ripples
Their body flows over
They live in a garden
Underneath the garden
And graze upside down
And live upside down
You can get there only
By turning away
To see the Sun

In peripheral flowers
At the edge of vision
You get there only
By turning away
Into the trough
To dunk your head
To see the light
Come in through the filter

OBJECT AIRLOCK

frantic typographical device of → NO SEATBELTS MOTHERFUCKER!! & cross the median or media membrane into the subgarden A TIGHTENING SHELL the ambulatory fragments of sundial time refract and light through the windshield fracture which fast gave way to ONE BOOT + lightning rails + lightning rod + lightning sun that the fuckers somehow found a way to monetize THE BOY WHO ENTERED THE MARE AND DIDN'T LEAVE he spent years inside there gently chewing the purple translucent walls and watching the sun come thru in his eyes AND THINK OF THE PAST "an escapist fantasy" which lives in a small fragment of dust crossing the light of the room in the future of time WHEN I OPEN MY MOUTH the petals folded . . .

there is no one in the subgarden but OUR VARIEGATED SELF.

we found a way to behead our flowers.

- -

and we become elsewhere

in here

out there

where can

.

a body

augment

the miracle failures   a body

we saw

in the garden

you can get there only
by tugging a network of roots so
heads of leaders cleave off
in vine or recyclable plastic
nets to decompose slow
or else quick in a plastic
raised composter w/ added
moisture and slits and
augmented RED WRIGGLERZ
the junk letters for better
insurance with mailer
windows and blood smeared
on the throne removed
in the name of microbial oxygen
AND SPREAD WHAT'S LEFT
to consume years of manure
and property seized
can we get there only
by turning away

- -

A language with no capitals. The subgarden is leaderless, comprised of tentacle weeds. Leaves of dandelion, beards of the dead. Is compost a form of restorative justice, a reprogramming of biological or learnéd code. Does subgarden mean watching my former abuser's head decompose, with worms crawling in and out of sockets while I contemplate comfort. What is power? It's a garden. A gallery. A golf course.

THE SAME RELATION OF THE ANTECHAPEL TO THE GOTHIC CHURCH

& over the years
  the lines got smooth

               the lines got smooth   &
                 so did the stoopid brainy
          wrinkles of trauma ironed
         like a grayish broke revolution
           -nary neural architectural
             vein rerouting
                an over-
                   turned cop car
                 made chasm of ribeye

    OR VESTIBULE OF ORNERY THOUGHT

                        a circle cathexis
                        a spot of time.

                  ----

is what I remember.
  is almost nothing,
is prosodic light flooding in thru glass
  staining the sofas & imported rugs
waiting for horses or visible breath of sunlight
  to enter again and so blood
makes the body
move before it's living
suffusing
the amniotic waters
like an opaque portentous mist

[& eye will be a father]

,   ,   ,

this recollection, I reframe it
       & it becomes a certain course
       of my made brain
       nostalgic intimation
       of cyberpunk circuitry
        a sentiment construed
       with analog wiring
       THE HOLY PROSODIC
       RECOLLECTED surface
of glass or silk or ornate frieze by the ceiling a milky book or arcade
bound by violence or waxed thread
(like everything else
       I reframe mine knowledge
       thru a shattered windshield

                                 I'm waiting
                                 for horses

un*sightly* things

the antechapel
was a forest
w/ deer all wearing
their winter coats
& I bow before the rabbit like a filmy gauze
       draped over the landscape

a narthex, nave or emblem
a spot of time

is what I remember,
is almost nothing
is a recursive splatter of blood
rewinded leaving the floral wallpaper
returning to its droplets
to its stream &
to its fleshy neck
the jugular vein and slashed
vagus nerve
a body poised in the chair
gazing into glass

"good bye to my sweet birth-place"
I witness my own memory
motherfucker
im waiting for horses

In this instance the form of the arch of the window, the character of the moldings, and the arrangement of the tracery, are better than was usual at that late period.

I LIVE IN THE SURPLUS
& PROJECT AN INFANT'S SWEAT
ON THE SUPPRESSED SHEET OF
MORNING.

ROMANTICISM IS

learning to see again is learning to follow the fan again is learning to shape one's lips into a grin again in response to external stimuli again is coughing while ingesting a small amount of dust again is looking in the mirror again and seeing yourself stare back in the mirror again a spider hanging and opening its furry legs again bisected by the window shutting is pressing down on the eyelids again like a corpse or sleeping child again to see utter darkness or webs of red and purple lines again as the case may be is thoughts like clouds forming and deforming in your head again is one strawberry hair longer than the other again is an outline of sweat again is vomiting up a necessary part of expunging use again is pressing down on your belly again or seeing a redness arise on skin again or producing tears for the first time again to bloom like a bloodprick in the corner of the eye and following the fleshtrench down to the ears again to see snow again or to never see snow again as the case may be is to cross the border to home again for the first time seeing maple syrup shops with roofs caving in again is to produce something for the first and last time in this world not involving an exchange of currency or worldly goods again to produce mucus again to produce waste for the first time in the form of fecal matter that contains history again and I hold on tight to your tiny hand

BOOK FOURTH
"Summer Vacation," or, Utopia

* * * * * * *

 * * * * * *

* * * * * * *

In the summertime, I would get high by Six-Mile Creek, annotate Wordsworth, sit by the waterfall near the abandoned factory, and scream. The churning water would cover the sound—both its symbolic content, and its varying dynamics. It was a good life. I'd eat olives. I'd put my feet in the water. I dreamed of a utopian society that would guarantee everyone the right to healthcare, subsidized travel to visit friends who lived far away, a garden, chickens (if desired), a watermelon-colored kiddie pool (if desired), and a skate ramp in the backyard (mandatory). There would be no more than two hours of work a day—with a designated thirty-minute break in the middle to stare into the rainbow prism of the nearby waterfall, astrally projecting one's body into faraway geographies via a public infrastructure of bluish lightning. We would all be inventors, innovating methods to keep our friends safe. There would, of course, be no cops, no presidents, no prisons, nor landlords. Enclosure would exist, but it would not be predicated upon property and discernible lines; rather, it would take various forms of amorphous provisional attachments, pink clouds crossing over each other surrounded by crumbling stone fences that were, themselves, comprised of the earth, and that would, themselves, collapse and eventually form different fences. Over time, the necessary gallows that allowed us to arrive here would become hard to name; our own children would carry it in leather trunks under boxes of old clothing in the back of their skulls, collecting mold; their children would know it only through the way it occupied the spiral chain of their DNA. It would never be a particularly simple revolution. But we would be happy. And when I would see my feet in the water, they would look like the feet of someone else.

IT IS THE GOAL OF THE MENACE TO ABSOLVE US OF MEANING

what.

moss.

grew.

from.

you

a host in a rock of BOVINE CONSCIENCE a celestial atom under the tongue of how the stars slid across the room & formed tangible lines on my chest, SURFACE BETRAYAL! you have to close your eyes to see the complex webs of intestinal longing, pay what you want, stand where you want, blue air thru your hair and access the server on your personal device, a trillium seal, a tulip we're after, a fern we swallow, we compost our sadness until the outline changes and I'm in the basement with the jug in my hand------

to.

have.

grown.

up.

again.

TO BE RELENTLESS AND FURTIVE IN OUR GAZE! a glacial shiver a red shag-carpeted coffin making its way down the river through cyclical gaps in the nimble current, *screaming at a waterfall and expecting a response.* I agree w/ the wind in me and the needle out of me the broken cellar window we swam into the foundation of the abandoned utility shed hung by the lord of capital on the granite hill, we kissed under asbestos with blue shivering lips. unless?

TO HAVE GROWN UP AGAIN. To return to silence and digital meadows with the innocence of a headless dove who brays her way into experiential loss. I was here once before in this text before you. I swallowed tadpoles and swam with no ambivalence, a footless swain on a bermless hillock. The brain of a worm and the wine gone through me.

SCAN   OVER.   OPEN.   WATER.

Each June I was plagued by the feeling that I was in fact already dead, a fecund corpse making its way through the yellowy alley of days . . . I fell asleep one night and dreamed my chest became a field of wheat with apple trees growing from each of my nipples, my belly button a small pond in which sunfish swam . . . There was a man ploughing the field, singing to himself under his breath and I could barely hear him over the sound of the motor, he turned at a corner, turned once more, and then saw my face and stopped the engine. His face was a smaller version of my own, looking back, sort of smiling, almost laughing. Monoculture of the torso. I was ecstatic, permeable, and dead, and I was the Sun.

AND

     LIGHT

          POURED

               FROM MY

       EYES

     AND PAINTED

           THE SOIL

CLOSURE DIAGNOSIS

I don't want to live in this world
I want to live in the heifer bellies
Sanctified under the overturned
Plastic motor oil container resting at the crest
Of the stinky bog, the space within
Which various forms of vibrant life
Do their fucking thing and eat each other
In a manner which seems emotionally detached
But devoted, a beaver-like ganglion or brain
Leaking fluid on a ceramic platter
Another planet, a better garden
A better poem or a future where I don't feel the need
To write poems or I write them
From a space of HEALTHY CONTEMPLATION
On a reclining chair drinking light beer in the backyard
Rather than endless desperation several times
A year & an empty stomach
Of useless labor they don't even
Call labor, what we bring is useless
In the best-case scenario
We redefine use

it is impossible / to be alone

SKATE OR DIE YOU DUMB MOTHERFUCKERS

Silverbird necrosis I'm drinking a negroni in an inflatable pool. The body consumed on its way to the soil. What's under the garden within the laundry. Trace amounts of semen on discernible garments, I gaze with a taciturn smile to the busy road (don't look away). I want to migrate from civic life with my spouse and daughter and learn nollie heels. I want to own a miniature Jersey cow (don't look away). I regurgitate reason from my open chest THE FEELING IN ME THE NEST BESIDE ME (don't look away) outside the motel without a key. I'm tired OK.

BOOK FIFTH
The Illegible City

A giant serpentine menace built by the military slithers its way through the alleys, gazing through tenement windows and enacting face scans, a ribbon of red crossing each assemblage of familial eyes. In the city, there is an intimacy. The people press their noses against the dirty glass.

And within each eye socket of the snake is a cockpit. One pilot, a new recruit, sits in the left eye and controls the mechanical functions of the internal organs and sperm duct—wielding a joystick, caked with decades of fingerprinted residue, saliva and vomit; the right-eye pilot controls the primary motor movements.

The serpent has no rectum but can reproduce. Its eggflap plants seeds
penetrating six inches into algorithmically chosen plots of land;
within the seed, a spermbody grows & ruptures the fleshy canal,
emitting from the dirt in a byzantine sunlight pattern
that begets more serpents, blades speed up, velocity increases . . .

By the time we get up in the morning, the police have beheaded our goats, leaning their bodies like tripods against our garden shed, a warning written in blood on our barn.

We panic. We get in the truck and begin driving. We approach the highway exit, notice a pummeling sound on the road behind us—"What the fuck," you say, "sounds like a bowling alley."

We pull over. I leave the cab. I walk around back and see the goat heads attached to the bumper— eyehooks driven into their skulls and connected with chains. I stare. Their slitted eyes stare back. We continue driving.

We pull over at a rest stop. I ask for a key and enter the bathroom, look at myself in the mirror. From the dollar dispenser, I buy a condom and a packet of Horny Goat Weed.

My reflection is laughing but I am not.

I begin coughing and my tear ducts open. A mass of leathery ribbons crawls up my throat, a humming in me until my esophagus fills. I keep coughing. I puke. A stream of small serpents pours into the sink.

it is impossible / to be apart

~ ~

Without the city, the country does not exist. Without you, I do not exist, nor do my memories or this baby or book. I am showering meaninglessly in a room where a dream visibly accumulates distanced from the endlessly beautiful feeling of being pressed against your ass and feeling you breathe while you sleep or are pretending to sleep as Baby Mae coos to herself and wakes in terror and sees the ceiling fan and closes her eyes. It is June again like always in my poems and the window unit is humming.

Between me and the city? *Your body beside me in bed, a limb protruding through your undulating back, begging to get out. In your stomach? A sun. A swamp.*

Between me and the city? *Baby Mae undulating from the other side of the curtain & her body curtailing, a small civilization of expired milk accumulating in the folds of her neck. To facially signify joy before muscles are linked to feeling. I drive to Target for the billionth time that day and have the line "when you open up" stuck in my head—remembering what it is to be human, not me*

FROM HUMANITY DIVORCED THE HUMAN FORM

and within the swamp an ABJECT BECOMING the
fingers callow the men who sit on the curb & spit brown
liquid in the sawed-off bottom of the Pepsi can I HOLD
OVER FLAME can I betray my elders & pray that each face
I pass on the street will go blank indefinitely A WHITE
OR BLUE ORB held up by a body moving to quarantine
the alley with gutters of piss of definite desire I beggar
the water I beggar the power the prolific bundles of
Downy to fill carts and chest cavities EVERY BODY IN
LONDON definitely hobbling over hobbling under the air
ventilators rigged up with cigarette butts THE GERMS

within the city
within the city
my innards entwine
a history like DNA
a prophetic gut
or an AK-47 hung
on the wall in yr expanded crisis
a suburban mancave
amongst the darts and homebrewed pilsner
a toxic wind or voiceless worm comes in my left ear
to wind its way thru the folds of my brain
and come out the other side
on the other side
a gray matter
like a microwaveable wrap
the membrane chews within the city

and within the city the echoing sadness of the body underwater.

Fish shift by, the contiguous universes separated by thick, shatterproof glass, like that which comprises my daddy's helmet. The enraptured ruptures. The lightning contagious. The deer still swimming. The kittens were born here down below, mewling thru hallways of manmade light. They made one of my hands a machine. Then, another. Then, the injection, and when my voice emerged, it wasn't mine. When the cats crawl through holes in the walls, what mazes do they enter, and from what source does the light emerge? The men follow with axes and paint them alive. We dreamed in neon. We made a promise.

BOOK SIXTH
Childhood or Whatever

THE SMALL ELUSIVE THISTLEDOWN LOOPS-THE-LOOP LIKE A STUNT PLANE IN SLOW MOTION AS IT SLOWLY GOES TO EXTREME HEIGHTS AND SWAYS TO THE GROUND

& the West River churned, and the economy flowed.

my internal body felt distinct, somehow, from my emotional state. hallowed bower shaping the pome. I hadn't heard of masturbating. we went riding once when it was forty below. a meadowy vacuum of blue survival. we knocked our feet against the ski-lift bar. I hadn't hit puberty. to make blood continue flowing. I was homeschooled, a fluid circuit. you kick to stay alive and stay in motion, from then until now, from now until what. in the moment of writing, to survive time and what violence does to the body. with who I saw when I saw the mirror. a flawed vehicle lacking headlights. to pretend my organs didn't exist. to drive in the rain & in the dark. at odds with how the others saw me. *little shit* as prelapsarian subject, relational shaping by the hand of god. compulsory yoga every Monday. make yrself opaque to live. instant messaged nightly with a beautiful boy. didn't name it love or him a boy. commuted from my town through several others. rode a bus painted like a holstein cow. pubes emerged slow with the towel removed, I never knew it had no name. the prelude is a frame. these were the fields assigned to me. drink black tea, go back to sleep. look out the window while the oldies play. drowned in affection. obsessed simultaneously with "meadows" and with "gardens." the depths of kinship. acted like a shit & was hated for it. the West River churned and the economy flowed. ski shops & heroin deaths. pubs painted red and white like barns

*   *   *   *   *   *   *

    *   *   *   *   *   *

*   *   *   *   *   *   *

In the year 4036, I purchased a camera. I became obsessed with how light moved through semi-transparent surfaces: from the sun, thru the water and algae surface skimmers, thru the lens and aperture thru the viewfinder mirror, into mine eye, into mine optic nerve & visual cortex, into mine posterior interior frontal gyrus and Pars triangularis, mine spinal cord neurons, mine caffeinated sweating hand and fingers with soiled nails at 9:53 am hungover avoiding productive futuristic occupation and regularized bowel movements, into the Freudian vision of the consciousness as a city with continual traffic, into keystroke mechanism made thru violence, an electric signal through insulating layers, to make words, TO MAKE DIRT

to make a stonewall fence

to make a sto ewall fence

to mae a stonewll fence

to ma a stnewall fece

tomkatonewallfce

toa**tonewll*fce

to%**^wll*fc

t%**^*fc

t*fc

,,,

,,

,

,

,

,

,

,

,

,

,
,
,
,
,
,
,
,
,
,
,
,
,
,
,
,
,
,
,
,
,
,
,
,
,
,
,
,
,
,
,
,
,

ACCESS POINT

bottom-left corner of filthy
dream in shack or house
or mansion rip shag carpet at
forty-five-degree angle & lift
what's left and brush
away glitter reverberate
time & shards of stripped
bolts and dig until nails
are dirty & enter the crawlspace
the light breaks narrative
and eviscerates carpus wind
to fuck up time gravitational
capital authoritarian vacuum
of VOICE-ACTIVATED BRITISH DEATH
I dream of the access point
in the secret passage
in the old home of a dead friend
whose name I forgot
I write to bite hands and cut into flesh
and hang filthy fuckface men
how they once hung me
the Chainsawer of Sun to chop
the sentences into Disagreeable Arrangements
to fuck the showhome
into oblivion and eat dirt
from the unstained subfloor
EVERYTHING YOU LOVE ABOUT GEOGRAPHIC SPACE
/ IS THAT WHICH RESISTS ASSIMILATION
the greenery makes its way slowly down the fence
it is June
I'm tired of being sad as fuck

DELEUZE AND GUATTARI ARE FLOATING DEAD IN THE RIVER AND I PROD THEM GENTLY WITH A STICK

Am I PACIFYING TRANSPARENT LUNG or do
my contours shift into more strident vengeance
against the mouse exiting the fridge halo and
crossing the porch and into the crack of sweltering
crawlspace and onto the lawn where it enters from
the hole BENEATH THE COMPOST the worms
enter and lose their bodies and gain their bodies and

the
striated
garden
on
a
moon
itself

the cultural lawn made a measure of how we
approach semantic messiness to pull from roots
and kill what's unwieldy and if we have a mess at
all it's in SMALLISH CONTROLLABLE PATCHES
an ivy a briar an authoritarian herbaceous layer
a golden retriever gleefully shitting WHILE ITS
HAUNCHES TWITCH and sipping Twisted Tea as
the days run by

we
gave
the
chickens
human
names

Dorothy Sidney Little Lucia or Lucy or Daddy's
Little Layer or Bertha Roberta or My Breakfast
Maker Purveyor of Shit and Calcified Fragments
a Made Language like the Remnant Smear and
Protruding Straw that Clings to the Egg

that
language
clings
to
the
inside

※　　　　※　　　　※　　　　※　　　　※　　　　※　　　　※

　　※　　　　※　　　　※　　　　※　　　　※　　　　※

※　　　　※　　　　※　　　　※　　　　※　　　　※　　　　※

At the creek, sometimes I would get on all fours, crawling through a tunnel that would take me to a small space directly behind the waterfall. I tried screaming in there, and even though no one could hear me, I felt safe. I felt the spray of water, the warmth of refracted sun. The coldness of stone. I called it the Green Room.

alone in the green room sipping kombucha. alone in the city the cellophane quiver. alone in the green room a suitcase of water. alone in the bathroom calling my mother, the fall of the west the green room surrounded with xmas tree lights that blink in a pattern disturbed by the intermittent burnout of power, the commas continue and rivet for miles, across from the creek and beyond the river, prime the engine and pull the generator and the flashbulbs break & THE SERPENT IS THERE suspended in air. alone in the green room I sing an enclosure, the inside of the cat like a pie full of meat, barbed wire atop the chainlink the suspended human fingers and chipmunk appendages, an empire conceived via what is dug in a trench and built and concealed. alone in the aqueduct the basin arcade. alone in the green room between fuct and knotted. alone in the green room the umbilical carpet littered with cannabis ashes sucking sneakers and ankles sucks the knees they see legs through the ceiling in the supply chain quadrant indexed to approximate demand of the town to traffic the rational green room sewn in seats and lung and sequined song and siphoning gas SUCK & SPIT & COUGH cough alone in the green room the eisenhower highway the programmed mourning the cigarette coffee the shredded wheat, standing in the yard with a bathrobe & your visible breath & the hounds circle round & a city designed with violence in mind. alone in the green room greening the sheets for the next guest in attendance in the vapor of days it is nice to meet you go fuck yourself. the green room designed with optimal acoustics upon which doves hover before they spiral and fall. alone in the green room I hold in my friends alone, I hold it all in like an aquarium filter or the calcium deposits or shit or stretchmarks on a freshly laid particularly belabored egg. the mouse feces littered the counter and the bags of rice, there is no way out so I hold them in, I hold in Kina and myself and our creatures and varying fluids that fill my gut. alone in my green room I withhold my jaw: this is called a mechanism of control. alone in the green room before the performance. alone in the green room after the performance. alone in the green room during the performance...

end exchange of beer to LUNGBODYBIRTH a
hair arising within the surface the worms swim
in light like petals in water & end exchange
a SLUGINMYEAR to turn under move a
light the red-beaded flesh against the variegated
earth unbelievable in its varietal fungus a
FUGUESTATESKY a fernlike sentence end
exchange my ring finger grips the aluminum sweat
the appendage commingled with condensing
moisture the cellular fingers touch the towers &
touch the cracks in the earth pulsate momentarily
& disappear behind my EYETHEFOREST of red
swallows itself a blanket of milk that bears bodies
a furry star a chainlink interwoven when I shut my
eyes I think of infrastructure & the centuries that
align with creases in the earth the cats running
thru snow both ORIGINARYANDNOT return me
to the version of my body that is an iron-wrought
structure waxed in various FORMSOFFEELING
and discarded red scarves that create their own
gravities beyond the apex the wayback gear
of gars & snowy fauna turn over turn under

In this example the debased character usual at that period comes out more distinctly than in the previous example, the arch of the window has entirely lost any point, and the tracery is very confused and irregular.

BOOK SEVENTH
Love

SUBGARDEN LOVE POEM FOR KINA

NOTHING IS STATIC AND EVERYTHING IS ROOTED. I scan the vine, I put the coordinates in my Subgarden Navigator & kick back and E N J O Y T H E R I D E with a whorl of wind & composting leaves, the radio whirring in necrotic ears. If utopia is real it's a coop where we prance down a ramp in the morning W I T H E X C E S S I V E L I G H T and eat dried mealworms and relish in shade. I'm lying on the lawn thinking about vines and clouds and the utter endlessness of love, there's no other way to say it but so I write around it AND I ONLY GET THERE BY SHUTTING MY EYES! Lacan was wrong, it's a macular object lacking a center, it's a cloaca emitting both eggs and shit, it's an oven-fresh cookie with an uncooked nimbus A PERMEABLE AIRLOCK RESISTING CLOSURE of lines or sinewaves or hayseed fields for love is a mode of political existence, a serpent in the sewers who slithers from the lid. I'm sitting on the sofa, waiting for you. If utopia is real, it's stars inside a horse, the salvageable facets of art like a fractured hydrant watering the wounds of my garden flesh. The couch and the sweat. The world and what's left. We get drunk and we go to the movies.

SUBGARDEN LOVE POEM FOR MAE

(Who has shit herself
And stares at me
Or some silhouetted iteration
Of me

THE PRESSE / OF SELF DESTROYING

the time
preserved in
assem
bled
tubes

THE LONGISH NEEDLE IN A CREEK OF THIGH

you have to kill
the garden
to get there

THE FIFTH BOOK WAS TITLED "BOOK"

Literary form is a form of enclosure, an Inclosure Act of my conscious talons, a ludicrous sadness, a talent attrition where I shut my eyes, a lifting coffin, a heterosexual bower, a compulsory frame to the dream I'm in bed I'M IN BED BESIDE HIM a porno forest, a foreskin lip of fluorescent light & you rapidly turn & see the branches, resounding moon O you disappear forward, you feel your body lurch towards the sparkling present, in the way of the dozer's psychic mowing, smooth the trauma, the prophetic mistake of a cock in my mouth, language a monster I keep in my belly, a response to capital and vociferous sadness, alive in the Uber in the poetic line, ENCLOSE THE HUMAN FOR TERRIBLE SHIT, a web of poetics, a material basis, an email field where you hide the sender.

AFTER THE PRELUDE

holy city
in a silver skillet I
swallow twine
in my cat's stomach
a whirl outside
the whither leaves
other pools

AFTER THE PRELUDE

After the end, the edging wisdom, asleep on the sofa adorned in cats, after the murder, beyond the martyr, the machine core rumbling inside the cushion THE CRUNCH OF METAL the churning feathers and fiber-optic cables under my hometown rimming groundhog tunnels adjacent to gardens with the fur from deer on electric fences, the optometrist arrested for masturbation, I stare into the goggles, a financed future, a yellowy desert, a blue house ranch at the end of the road and you remember nothing, after the protest the kids are laughing, after the prelude, I hold prepositions, a life confined not by walls but by rows of men wielding switchblades who threaten to knife you if you leave the track—even when sleeping, even when bathing, your threadbare robe in late summer light—a cactus wisdom, the backroom unprogrammed, the dream unprogrammed, my backdoor union, I just want to do drugs and suck Robert Duncan's dick until I open the fridge and see a rat on the platter, roach variation, after the lily, after the cutscene, you settle back a second and sip your beer, the end of format, a ditch in my bed, a used VCR with worms within, a thorny tiara, I show up to the rally and can't get inside. I want a baby and I'm tired of dying. The garden a crime scene.

STICK A HUNK OF METAL WITHIN THIS FORM

I plug
the deer-sensor
into the camping
generator
& turn the dial
we walk to the water
we stick in our tongues
to swallow the droppings
of cyborg deer
we came to murder
the hoofprint moons
like a fucked-up heart
property rended
of blinking traffic
a continual summer
or surrender
when I shut my eyes
the ferns around me
we drive several miles in the truck
with a spider making
a web in the bed
it sways in the wind
the world makes forms
and the king makes fences
to keep us from killing
ourselves on the gorges
in the name of patrilineal virtue
and implied liability
call this number
if you want to die
the deer-sensor sings
the wind hits leaves

and we follow prints to a thicket
where the animatronic deer
built a living space
the nomadic creatures move each hour
their television blaring
their paisley couch where they sit
and drink coffee and watch Bambi and cry
a nuclear family produced
through the law of the father
we come for them quiet
we see them sleeping
the king made us killers
or we made the king
and I walk behind the buck
and slit his throat
and we poison the fawn
and crush the doe
and the eyes leave the sockets
there is no blood
there are only springs
and wire and gears
rollicking gently across makeshift bedding
we stare in the iris
we see the reflection
the wires hold
we see the king leave the bath
and water drips down
his lean white body
he sits on the edge of the tub
his balls hang limp
he shuts his eyes
and his tears start running
how do we kill
in the garden we're building

I'm inside *The Prelude*. It's hot in here

By the lake, by the river, in the dry slightly torn pages

That some guy keeps turning, the oil of fingers and ash

Marking the archive for decades. It hurts when he writes

When he presses the pen into my chest and ink pours

Out from the hole. But there's sun in here. There's trout in here.

And when I look into the water, I see my face.

IN THOSE FITS OF VULGAR JOY

Was it for this? The summer ended. The empty pool. The hapless lung. The first leaf strung limply on wool, the strings of dry flowers above the TV and crackling light from every side. The static happening, an attic of trauma, an akratic sparrow chokes on the grub and the fragments multiply in glorious shards of a chardonnay bottle. The ligament mouth. The lingering moth. The shivering hornet. The haptic feeling of what exists outside form and it swallows me whole on the tongue of a whale and I slobber wind and mix psilocybin mushrooms into homemade pesto. The accessible angel. The program remote. The nostalgic den. The room where you lived and ate and grew sofa blisters and the crumbs of saltines and nuggets lived beyond us. The summer ended. The burning mall. The normcore goblin. The loss of geography as a locus for selfhood. The loss of locusts. The hands behind glass. The feverish symptom. The joy like a mark of tendrils across your skin when you rise from the carpet O hallelujah I grasshopper organs. The plaid horizon.

ACKNOWLEDGMENTS

This book was written at 627 Hudson Street, Ithaca, NY, and at the First Dam of Ithaca's Six-Mile Creek.

Selections from this book originally appeared in *Afternoon Visitor, Denver Quarterly, Dreginald, mercury firs,* and Rob McLennan's *Spotlight Series.* Endless gratitude to the editors of these publications.

Some sections of this book were originally released as short, self-published pamphlets, and several of the poems were recorded and released through a spoken word / sound collaboration with Nick Scollard called *BOGMOM:* https://bogmom.bandcamp.com.

This book borrows language and images from the following texts: Matthew Holbeche Bloxam's *The Principles of Gothic Ecclesiastical Architecture, Elucidated by Question and Answer,* 4th ed. (1841); John Henry Parker's *ABC of Gothic Architecture* (1882); and Eugène Viollet-le-Duc's *Dictionnaire raisonné de l'architecture française du XIe au XVIe siècle,* 1st edition (1865).

In addition to Wordsworth's *The Prelude,* this book is indebted to the following artistic works: Leonora Carrington's *Down Below* (1943; reprinted by NYRB Classics, 2017); *Bioshock* (2K Games, 2007); various films by Stan Brakhage; Édouard Glissant's *Poetics of Relation* (trans. Betsy Wing, University of Michigan Press, 1997); *The Last of Us* (Naughty Dog, 2013); Bernadette Mayer's *Utopia* (United Artists, 1984), and *The Green Room* (dir. Jeremy Saulnier, 2015).

Thank you to the following people who read and responded to this manuscript in its various incarnations: Toby Altman, Evan Gray, Joe Hall, MC Hyland, Jeffrey Lance, Gina Gail Nutt, Michael Martin Shea, Tim VanDyke, and Kina Viola.

Thank you to my family—especially Kina Viola and Mae Magnolia Viola-Cain—for their unwavering support of my creative practices.

Thank you to everyone who contributed a blurb, and to the Action Books team for their care and attention.

ABOUT THE POET

Marty Cain is a poet from Vermont. He is the author of *Kids of the Black Hole* (2017) and *The Wound Is (Not) Real: A Memoir* (2022), both from Trembling Pillow Press, as well as a chapbook, *Four Essays* (Tammy, 2019). His individual works appear in *Best American Experimental Writing 2020, Fence, Poetry Daily, Denver Quarterly, Sink Review,* and elsewhere. He holds an MFA from the University of Mississippi and a PhD from Cornell University, where he wrote a dissertation on rural poetic community. He is currently a postdoc within the Humanities Scholars Program at Cornell, and lives with his spouse and daughter in Ithaca, New York.